Plant Life in Field and Garden

By Arabella Buckley

Plant Life in Field and Garden

Layout and Cover Copyright ©2013
All Rights Reserved
Printed in the USA

Published through CreateSpace

Table of Contents

CHAPTER I: The Shepherd's Purse 4

CHAPTER II: The Work Done by Leaves 7

CHAPTER III: The Story of a Turnip 10

CHAPTER IV: How a Seed Grows 13

CHAPTER V: Making New Seeds 16

CHAPTER VI: How Insects Help 22

CHAPTER VII: Seed-Boxes Which We Eat as Vegetables 26

CHAPTER VIII: The Cabbage Plant 29

CHAPTER IX: How Plants Defend Themselves 33

CHAPTER X: Wild Flowers and Garden Flowers 37

CHAPTER XI The Rose Family and its Fruits 41

CHAPTER XII: The Dead-Nettle and the Pea-Flower 45

CHAPTER XIII: Climbing Plants 50

CHAPTER XIV: How Plants Store Food 57

CHAPTER XV: Underground Vegetables 61

CHAPTER XVI: How Seeds Travel 64

CHAPTER I: The Shepherd's Purse

IT is seven o'clock on a lovely summer morning. Jump up and look out of the window. It is a shame to be in bed when the sun is shining so brightly, and the birds are singing, and the bees are flying from flower to flower.

Why are the bees at work so early? They want to gather the yellow pollen-dust from the flowers, and the dew helps them to wet it, so that they can roll it up in little balls. Then they pack these balls into a groove in their hind legs, and fly away to the hive. There they mix it with honey, and make it into bee-bread to feed the young bees.

See how busy that woodpecker is, under the elm tree. He is catching insects to carry home to his little ones, which have been hatched more than a week. Further away in the field is a thrush struggling with a big worm: I expect that he too is getting a breakfast for his family.

How busy they all are, and you in bed! If I were you I would get up and pull up some weeds in the garden. Then you will be of some use, and you can learn many interesting things, while you are at work.

Here is a weed, growing among the cabbages. Do you know its name? It is called "The Shepherd's Purse" because of its curious seed-pods. These grow on stalks up the stem of the plant, below the little white flowers. If you open one of them very carefully, you will find that there is a small bag on each side, which can be pulled away from the middle, when the pod is ripe, leaving the seeds hanging on a small division.

So the pod is a kind of purse, with two pockets, and we can pretend that the seeds are the shepherd's money.

Take hold of this plant, and I will tell you about its different parts. First look at the *root*. That always grows downwards into the ground. It has small rootlets growing out of it. The root and the rootlets all have tender tips, and they drink in the food of the plant out of the ground.

You know that your father puts manure into the earth before he sows his seeds, or plants his fruit trees. Then the rain sinks into the earth and takes the juice out of the manure. This makes a, rich drink for the roots to suck in, and so the plants grow strong.

SHEPHERD'S PURSE

Plant Life in Field and Garden

Next look at the *stem*. You can tell where it begins, for a tuft of leaves grows close to the ground. A root never has any leaves on it, so where the leaves grow must be the stem. The place where the stem joins the root is often called the *stock*.

Look carefully at this tuft of leaves. You will see that they do not grow exactly one above the other. The leaves in the upper row always grow just between the leaves of the lower row. And as the stem grows upwards, and the leaves are farther apart, they still grow so that they are not exactly one above the other.

Why do you think they grow like this? Because they want to get as much sun as they can. If they grew exactly one above the other, the upper leaf would keep the sun away from the lower one. But now they get as much as there is to be had.

You see then that a plant has a root which grows downwards to take in water out of the ground, and stems to grow upwards and carry the leaves up into the sunlight. What the leaves do we will learn in the next lesson.

CHAPTER II: The Work Done by Leaves

THE leaves want a great deal of sunshine and air, for they are busy all day long, making food. Have you ever thought how wonderful it is that plants can make their own food? You do not make your food, and no animals make their own food. All you eat has once been either an animal or a plant. In a cake, for instance, the flour comes from grains of wheat, the currants from a little tree, the sugar from the sugar-cane, the spices come from trees, and the candied peel from fruits.

The other things you eat are meat, fish, birds, vegetables, and fruits, and all these have once been alive.

Plants do not feed like this. Their roots take in water out of the earth, and other substances, such as lime, soda, and potash, dissolved in it. The leaves take in gases out of the air. But earth, air, and water are not living food. You or I could not live on them. The plant can.

The pretty green leaves we love so much work very hard. When the sun shines upon them they can turn the water and gases into living food, and this food makes more leaves, flowers, and fruits which we eat.

See how useful plants are! If they did not make food, there could be nothing alive in the world. Insects feed on plants, and birds feed on insects. Sheep feed on grass, and we feed on sheep. Rabbits feed on plants, and foxes and weasels feed on rabbits. If there were no plants, there could be no insects, no birds, no animals, and no men alive.

But this is not the only useful work which plants do. You know that if many people are shut up in a room, they use up the fresh air, and breathe back bad air, which is not fit to use again. Now plants want this foul air. They take it in through their leaves, and use a gas which is in it to help them to grow. So they not only turn gases into food for us to eat, but in doing this they use the bad air we send out of our mouths, and give it back to us fresh and pure. This is why it is so healthy to live in the country, where there are so many plants.

Plant Life in Field and Garden

You will find it very interesting to look at the leaves of plants, and notice their shapes, and how they are arranged on their stems so as to get light and air.

I think you must know the common Dead-nettle, which is so like a stinging-nettle but does not sting. It grows in the hedges, and has a pretty purple or white flower shaped like a hood. Its leaves are arranged in pairs all up the stem, and each pair stands exactly across the pair below it, so as to let in plenty of light.

(A) DEAD-NETTLE; (B) WOOD SORREL

The glossy green leaves of the ivy on the wall lie out flat, and have long stalks, so that they can stand out well into the air.

The leaves of the Nasturtiums in our gardens are shaped like a round shield. The leaf-stalk grows from under the middle of the leaf and is very long. So the leaf looks up straight to the sky, and gets plenty of light and air.

The leaf of the Horse Chestnut tree is divided into leaflets, so that it looks as if it were made of five leaves, and each leaflet is spread out to the light.

The leaves of the little Wood Sorrel, which children love to bite because it tastes sour, have three round leaflets like the Shamrock, and these leaflets droop down at night, or on a wet day, but stand up wide open when the sun is shining.

And now let us go back to our shepherd's purse. We have not yet looked for the flowers; they grow on stalks which come out between the leaf-stalks and the stem. On these stalks there are some smaller leaves and a good many seed-pods.

Above the seed-pods at the top of the stalk are some white flowers growing close together. They are so small that you can scarcely see the parts. But you can make out that they have four outer green leaves and four white inner leaves. In the next lesson we will learn more about these.

Gather six plants with different shaped leaves and notice how they grow upon the stem.

CHAPTER III: The Story of a Turnip

THE flowers of the Shepherd's Purse are very small, so we will get the flowers of another plant to help us to learn about them. If you can find, in the garden, a turnip plant that has run to seed, you will see that it has flowers very like those of the Shepherd's Purse, only they are larger, and yellow instead of white.

In both flowers there are four outer green leaves. These are called *sepals*. They form the cup or *calyx* of the flower. Then there are the four coloured leaves, which grow above the sepals. These are called *petals*. They make the crown or *corolla* of the flower. They are white in the Shepherd's Purse, and yellow in the Turnip flower. But in both flowers they stand in the form of a cross.

Next come six thin threads with little knobs on the top. Two of them are short, and four are long. These are called *stamens*. The knobs are called *anthers*, they are the dust-bags which hold the yellow dust or *pollen*. Lastly, in the middle of the flower, is the seed-box or *ovary*. In the Shepherd's Purse the ovary is shaped like a heart, in the Turnip flower it is a long pod.

The pods grow on little stalks down the stem. They once had flower-leaves round them. But these have withered away, and the pods have grown large.

Some of the best vegetables in your garden have flowers like these in the form of a cross, and with four long and two short stamens. Some, like the turnip and radish, have roots that are good to eat. In others, such as the cabbage and mustard-and-cress, we eat the leaves. In cauliflower and broccoli we eat the flowers.

Now let us go back to our turnip. What a splendid round root it has! You can find a kind of turnip growing wild in the lanes, but the root is hard—you would not like to eat it. Our turnips are good, because they have been grown in good ground, and had good food for hundreds of years, and only the best seeds are sown.

Now I daresay you think that, as we dig the ground and sow the seed, we ought to keep the turnip for ourselves. But there are a good many animals and insects which want their share. As soon as the turnip seed has sent up its first green leaves, a little beetle is there, ready to eat them. When its wings are closed it is not much bigger than the letter *O* in the title of this lesson. It has long hind legs and can hop very far, so it is called the Turnip Flea-beetle.

GARDEN TURNIP AND FLEA-BEETLE

In the winter these beetles sleep under the clods of earth, or under dead leaves. When spring comes they wake up, and feed on the Shepherd's Purse, or some other weed, which comes up early in the year. The mother flea-beetle lays her eggs under the leaves, and very soon the tiny maggots come out, and eat tunnels in them.

Plant Life in Field and Garden

In a fortnight they are fat. Then they fall to the ground, and wrap themselves up in their cocoon skin, just as the baby ants did in the ant-hill. In another fortnight they become little beetles.

By that time the early turnips are just sending up their first leaves, and the flea-beetles will hop a long way to eat them. So, when you get up some morning, you may find the turnip bed very bare, and if you have sharp eyes you may catch the little black shiny beetles which have done the mischief. A whole field of swedes or yellow turnips may be eaten down in this way.

If you clear away all the weeds early in the year, and rake the ground, so that the young turnips grow quickly, you may keep the flea-beetle away. But then other creatures are wanting their share. The turnip-weevil will lay her egg in the root underground, as the nut-weevil did in the nut in the tree (*see* Book I.). If you pull up a turnip with little lumps or *galls* on it, you may know that a weevil maggot has been hatched inside.

Then, when the large turnip leaves have grown, the pretty orange saw-fly will leave her eggs in them, so that the maggots eat them all away. Then the rabbit, if he can get in, will eat the tops, while the mice will nibble at the root. Lastly, if you grow turnips for seed, the pretty little green flower-beetle wants his share, and he eats the flower-buds.

So you see the turnips feed many creatures besides the sheep and ourselves. A good gardener enjoys learning how to keep these garden thieves away.

Bring the flowers of wallflower, stock, candytuft, penny-cress, turnip-flower, and shepherd's purse, and notice their likeness in the form and arrangement of their parts.

CHAPTER IV: How a Seed Grows

WE saw in the last two lessons that a plant has a root, stem, leaves, flowers, and seed-boxes. To-day I want to tell you how these grow.

If your teacher will let you make a little experiment, you can watch a plant yourself as it grows out of the seed. Get a saucer and a small piece of flannel. Put the flannel in the saucer, and pour water over it till it is quite wet. Then get someone to give you a pinch of mustard seed, and scatter it on the flannel. Put this on the windowsill, or on the table, and take care to keep the flannel wet. Then watch what happens.

The second day after you have sown the seeds, you will find that they are swollen and soft. They have sucked up some water, and are using it to grow. On the third day many of the seeds will have sent out a tiny white root, which will cling to the flannel.

The tip of the root will now suck in more water, and if you will open a seed you will find that it is splitting in half. Each of the two halves is going to be a leaf. But they are not green, they are still quite white, and you would not think that they were leaves.

When you go to school on the fourth morning you may find these two halves out of their coat. Some of them are white, but some are turning green above and purple below, and everyone would now call them leaves. They grow up on a stem, and the empty coat of the seed still hangs on the place where the stem and the root meet. Look well at the shape of these leaves, they are made of two rounds with a dent in the middle. They are the *seed-leaves* of the mustard plant. They have come out of the seed, and have used the food that was in it, to spread themselves out, and rise up into the sunlight. Now as the light pours down on them, they turn green, and can make their own food out of the water and gases, which the roots suck in. For the root has now many rootlets and root-hairs on it, as you will see if you will pull one out of the flannel.

In a few days a green tip shows between the two seed-leaves, and grows up, opening out into two more leaves. These again have a little bud growing between them, which spreads out into other leaves, and so the plant goes on getting larger.

But the new leaves are quite different in shape from the seed-leaves. They are long, and are cut up into five leaflets, one large one at the tip, and two small ones on each side.

What you have seen happen to the mustard seed on the flannel is just what happens to every seed you sow in the ground. First it swells, when the warm rain reaches it. Then it puts out a tiny root. The seed-leaves stretch themselves out, their stem grows, and they creep out of their coat, and find their way above ground.

There they turn green in the sunlight, and begin to work up nourishing food. With this food they make fresh stems and leaves, till they grow into big plants, or even trees.

Another pretty experiment you can make is to soak a haricot bean in warm water, and put it on the top of some earth in a pot. Keep the earth moist and watch the bean, as you did the mustard seed. It will take longer to grow. It may be nearly a week before the root finds its way into the earth, and another week before the big green seed-leaves break out of the seed-coat.

A BEAN GROWING

It is very curious to watch the root. First it sends out only one rootlet. Then several more grow out, till the bean looks like a big spider with long legs. The heavy bean still lies on the earth, while the stem goes on growing. So the stem forms an arch, with the seed at one end, and the root at the other. At last the seed-leaves grow thinner as the plant uses the food in them, and the stem is strong enough to lift them, so that they stand up in the air. They do not leave the seed-coat down below, as the mustard seed did. They carry it up with them, and it dries and falls off at the top. Then you can see the new bud, between the seed-leaves, which soon opens out into real leaves.

Grow mustard seed on damp flannel. Soak a haricot bean in warm water for one night, and then keep it on very damp earth in a flower-pot.

CHAPTER V: Making New Seeds

WE left our plants, at the end of the last lesson, growing green leaves in the sunlight. Now they go on very quickly. Their roots take in water from the ground, and the leaves take in gases from the air.

When the plant has made plenty of roots, stems, and leaves, it begins to store up food for making flowers, in which new seeds will be formed. This is a very important work, for seeds are needed to grow up into new plants, and so many are destroyed by birds and insects or stifled by other plants that, if there were not plenty, the plants would die out.

So the seed-box, or ovary, is very carefully protected. It grows right in the middle of the flower, where it can be closely wrapped up in the bud. Even when it grows below the flower, as in the honeysuckle, the sticky tip is always safe inside the bud.

Gather a Primrose and Buttercup in the field, and a flower from the row of Peas in the garden, and look for their seed-boxes. In the middle of the butter-cup flower you will find a great number, shaped like pears standing upside down, with their stalks upwards, and in each of these seed-boxes there is the beginning of a little seed.

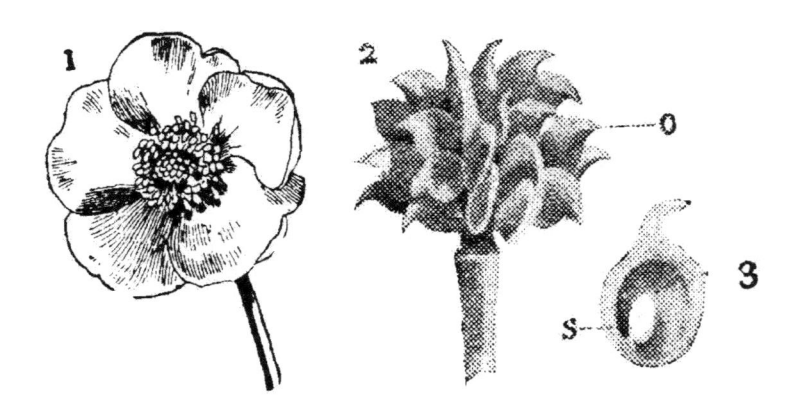

BUTTERCUP

You will have to pull the yellow crown off the Primrose before you can see the little round seed-box sitting in the green cup. It has a tube growing out of it with a round knob on the top.

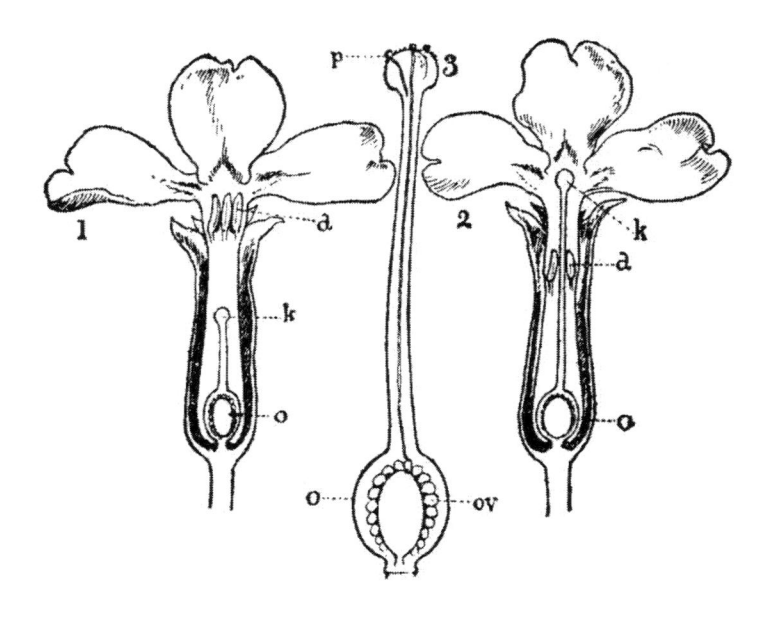

PRIMROSE FLOWERS

In the Pea-flower you will find one single pod inside the flower-leaves, and it has a long beak on the tip. When you open the pod you will see seven or eight white balls inside it, which are the baby peas. If you can cut open the seed-box of the primrose, you will find the same kind of balls, but very small indeed. These balls are soft and transparent. You can crush them with your fingers easily. They are not yet real seeds, but only bags of juice, called "ovules." Before they can grow into hard seeds, they must use some of the yellow grains out of the dust-bags which grow round them.

This is why the seed-boxes have tips, and beaks and knobs. The *tip* of the buttercup pods, the *beak* at the end of the pea-pod, and the *knob* at the top of the primrose-tube, are all sticky. The yellow grains stick to them like

17

flies on fly-paper. Then the grains burst and send some juice down to the ovules in the seed-box, and turn them into real hard seeds.

As you go home pick any flower you see, and try to find its seed-box. You may perhaps pick a Poppy in the cornfield. That has a fine large seed-box, like a covered cup, with holes under the cover. When the seed-box is ripe, and hangs down its head, the seeds fall out at the holes. There are so many you could not count them.

You may pick a Violet, and when you have taken off the coloured leaves, you will find a very curious seed-box. For the tube, and the sticky knob at the top, are just like a bird's neck and head. The dust-bags which fit close round the seed-box are a lovely orange colour.

If you can find a pretty purple flower called the Marsh Mallow, you will see that the seed-box is like a round flat cheese, with a long tube standing up in the middle. This tube has eight or twelve red sticky points; there are a great many yellow stamens round it. Country children often call the seed-boxes of the mallow "cheeses," when they are ripe and the long tube has fallen off.

But very likely you may pick a Daisy or a Dandelion. Then you will be puzzled, for you will not find a seed-box in the middle. This is because a daisy or a dandelion is not one flower, but a great many flowers crowded together in one head.

DANDELION

Take a dandelion flower-head to pieces, and you will find that each tiny flower will come away from the rest. There are more than a hundred in one dandelion head. Take one of these florets in your hand and have a look at it. At the bottom there is an oval bag, that is the seed-box. On the top of it there are some fine hairs, these are the sepals. Then there is the yellow crown with a long strap to it. Inside the crown come the stamens, with very long dust-bags, which cling round the tube. On the top of the tube stand two yellow sticky horns.

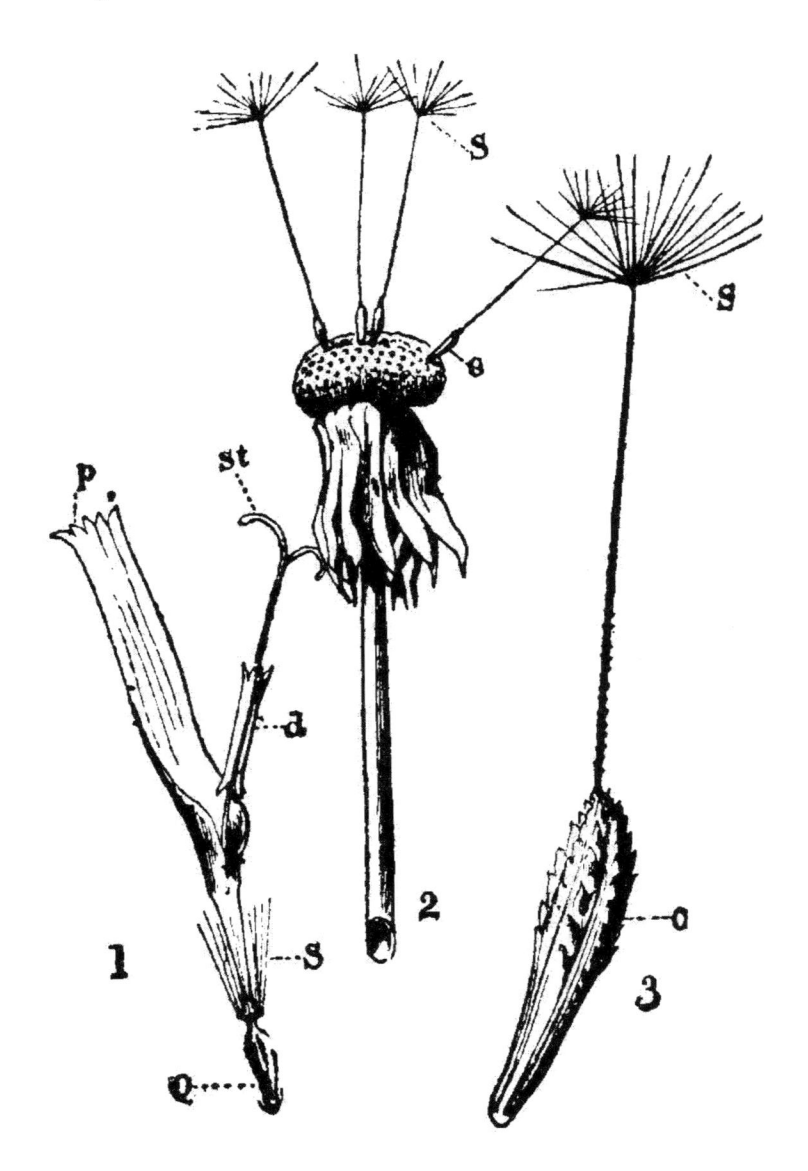

PARTS OF A DANDELION

So you see this tiny thing is a whole flower, growing with its companions on the dandelion head. The daisy is the same, with some little differences. See if you can make that out for yourself.

Find the seed-boxes of the pea, wallflowers, shepherd's purse, buttercup, primrose, poppy, marsh-mallow, and dandelion.

CHAPTER VI: How Insects Help

AS soon as the sun begins to warm the earth you may look out for spring flowers. If you have any damp ditches near you, you may find in March the Marsh Marigold in flower. This is a plant with hollow stems and dark green leaves shaped like a heart, and notched round the edge. It has large bright yellow flowers, which children often call "king-cups."

MARSH MARIGOLD

The yellow cup has only one set of flower-leaves. and inside it there are a great many dust-bags and seed-boxes. If you take off one of these seed-boxes and look on each side, you will find a little hollow with some honey in it.

The bees are very eager to get this honey, as it is so early in the year that there are very few plants in flower. They want too some of the pollen dust to make bee-bread for the baby-bees. The early flies too are in search of food. If you watch a bed of king-cups on a sunny day, you will see a number of bees and flies settling on the flowers.

They fly from flower to flower sipping a drop in each, and as they rub against the dust-bags, they carry the pollen-grains with them.

We saw in the last lesson that plants cannot make seeds unless the pollen grows downwards into the seed-box, and we find by experiments that they make better seeds when the pollen-grains come from another flower. So the bees do the flowers good, by carrying the pollen, in return for the honey that the plants give to them.

You are sure to find somewhere in the lanes in March a pretty little yellow flower like a star, with shining heart-shaped green leaves. It is the Lesser Celandine, and has a cup of five green sepals, and a crown of eight or ten yellow petals. Flies and bees come to it in numbers, for it has a drop of honey at the thin end of each petal, in the middle of the crown.

If you dig up a bit of this plant, you will find some white lumps growing among the roots. Each of these has a small bud at the top, and will grow into a plant if you put it into the ground.

Another flower already out in the fields is the common yellow Coltsfoot, a very tiresome weed to the farmers. It has a long creeping stem, and spreads very quickly underground. It has a flower-head, like the dandelion, made of hundreds of tiny flowers. This head grows on a fluffy stem which is covered with pink scales. The leaves do not grow till after the flowers are over.

Look carefully at the flower-head. You will find about forty tiny round flowers in the middle. They have dust-bags in them, and a large drop of honey. Round these stand about three hundred little flowers, each with a long yellow strap, and inside each of these outer flowers is a seed-box with two sticky horns. The bees and flies creep over these outer florets to suck the honey from the flowers in the middle, and on their way back they bring some pollen and leave it on the sticky horns.

And now, if you can find in the hedges the Cuckoo-pint or Arum I will show you a real trap for insects. It is a plant with a green pointed hood, and a purple club sticking up in the middle. We used to call it "Lords and Ladies," but many children call it "Parson-in-the-pulpit." In spring this plant has a very strong smell. When the flies smell it, they crawl down the purple club to look for honey.

1. ARUM OR CUCKOO-PINT; 2. THE COLTSFOOT

On their way they pass a row of stiff hairs which bend down with their weight and let them pass. Then they come to a ring of red dust-bags which are not yet open. Next they pass some useless seed-boxes and reach at last the true seed-boxes with sticky points.

Now they have come to the bottom, and they look for some honey. Alas! There is none there. Then they try to get back. But the stiff hairs will not bend upwards, and they are prisoners. They are shut in for a day or two, and then the sticky points of the seed-boxes wither, and each gives out a drop of honey. So the flies have not been cheated. At the same time the dust-flags burst, and the pollen dust falls on the flies. Then the stamens and the hairs wither away and the flies can get out again.

As they pass the withered dust-bags, they brush off any pollen-grains which remain, and have plenty on their backs to carry to another flower-trap.

You can see this for yourself if you will look for the Parson-in-the-pulpit, and choose two plants, one young one with the dust-bags full, and one old one in which they are withered.

Look for marsh marigold, lesser celandine, coltsfoot, and arum or cuckoo-pint.

CHAPTER VII: Seed-Boxes Which We Eat as Vegetables

WHEN the seed-boxes of plants are ripe we call them "fruits." I daresay it seems strange to you to call a pea-pod a fruit. But if you think of all the other fruits you know, you will find that they are all seed-boxes.

The apple is the seed-box of the apple-blossom. The gooseberry holds the seed of the gooseberry plant. The nut is the fruit of the nut-tree. The acorn is the fruit of the oak.

In peas and broad beans we eat the seeds out of the fruit. But in French beans and scarlet-runners we eat the whole fruit, seed-box as well as seeds. If you walk round a kitchen garden I think you can find one, and perhaps two, vegetables of which we eat the whole fruit.

In most gardens there is some corner where the dead leaves and rubbish are heaped up to make a hot-bed. Earth is thrown over the heap, and cucumbers and vegetable marrows are grown there. You will see at once that cucumbers and marrows are fleshy seed-boxes, for they are full of seeds.

Have you ever looked at the flowers of the Vegetable Marrow? They are as large and beautiful as many garden flowers. I want you to notice something curious in them.

If you look at several flowers you will see that they are not all alike. They all have a pale green cup, with five long points, and a grand yellow crown. But some, which are very big, have the beginning of a young marrow just under the green cup while others, which are smaller, have nothing but the stem under the cup. In a few days the young marrow will have grown bigger. But the flowers which have no marrows under them will be fading away.

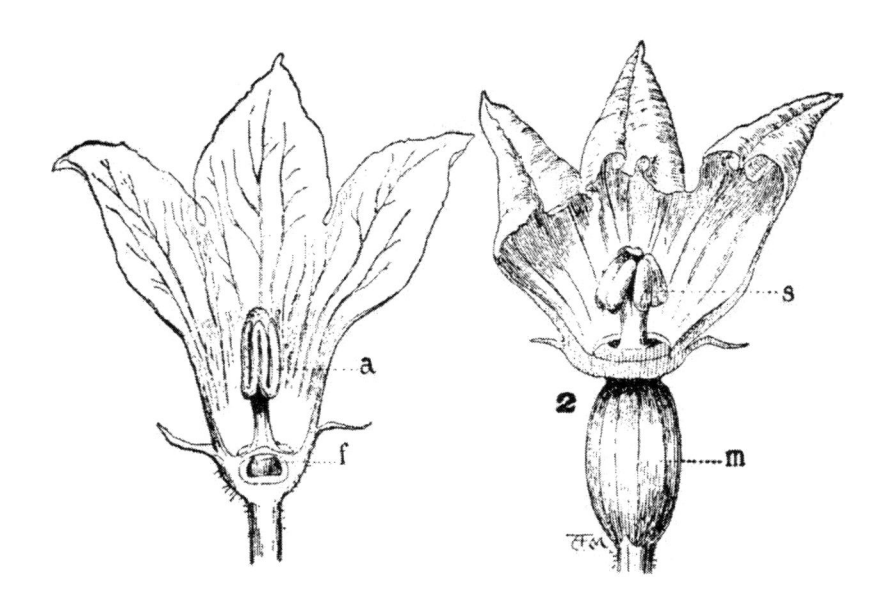

VEGETABLE MARROW FLOWERS

Look inside the fading flowers. You will see some curious twisted pouches full of yellow pollen-dust, but you will not find a sticky knob in the middle. Then look at the big flower at the top of the young marrow. Inside that flower you will find some sticky lumps, and most likely some yellow dust on them. So you will know that these lumps are the top of the seed-box. But you will not find any dust-bags in *this* flower.

So you see that the vegetable marrow has its dust-bags in one flower and its seed-box in another. How can the yellow grains get from one flower to the other to make the seeds grow?

Here the insects help. We found them troublesome when they spoilt the turnips, but now, they are going to be useful.

Inside each marrow flower there are some juicy folds, which the bees and flies love to nibble, to get the sweet juice. When they press into the flower to bite the folds they rub against the pouches and carry off some yellow grains on their backs. Then they go into the bigger flower to bite the folds, and pass the sticky lumps on their way. The yellow grains stick on to the lumps, and so the ovules of the marrow get the pollen-food and are able to grow into seeds.

The Cucumber flowers are of two kinds, like those of the marrow. Perhaps now, you can guess why the gardener is careful to open his frames every day. He must not only let in the fresh air. He must also give the insects a chance to fly in to the flowers. For if they did not come, there would be no one to carry the pollen from one flower to the other. Some gardeners pick off a flower with dust-bags, and rub it against the sticky lumps of the large flower, and so do the same work as the insects.

Pumpkins, melons, and gourds have two kinds of flowers like the cucumber and marrow.

There is one more fruit which we eat as a vegetable, but I am not sure if you will have it in your garden. It is the beautiful tomato, which looks like a deep red apple. If you have not got it you should try to grow it. Cottagers often grow it in Devonshire, even when they have only a sandy path to plant it in.

Sow the seeds in a box in February, put a piece of glass over it, and keep it in the kitchen where it is warm. Then when the little plants have two or three leaves on them, put each plant in a small pot with some very sandy earth.

Keep the plants well watered, and in May put the pots outside the house in a warm corner. As soon as they are a little hardened you may scoop a deep hole in the bed, or path, under a sunny wall. Fill it with manure and earth, and put the plants in out of the pots. They will grow against the wall and give you fine tomatoes. Only you must be careful to keep off the slugs and snails, for they love the sweet tomato juice as much as we do.

When the fruits are big, if the weather is not warm enough for them to ripen out of doors, you may pick them and put them on the kitchen shelves and they will turn red and be fit to eat.

Bring the two kinds of flowers which grow on the vegetable marrow plant—also those of the cucumber. Bring in the fruit of a marrow, a cucumber, and a tomato.

CHAPTER VIII: The Cabbage Plant

WHEN the spring flowers are beginning to peep out in the fields, your father will be hard at work in the garden. In March, if not before, neat seed beds of cabbage, broccoli, Brussels sprouts, and cauliflower will have to be sown, for planting out by-and-by. Early turnips must now be sown in their rows, and radishes and mustard and cress may be grown for salad.

All these belong to the family which have flowers in the form of a cross. So you see this is a very useful family to gardeners. It gives us, besides the lovely wallflower, the purple stock and the sweet alyssum in our flower garden, as well as the watercress in the brooks.

But as soon as our cabbage plants begin to grow, we find that the insects, which are so useful in helping to make seeds, can do harm in a kitchen garden. Early in May, before the plants are very large, you will see the white cabbage butterfly with two black spots on her wings, flitting about the garden.

CABBAGE AND CABBAGE BUTTERFLY

Where do you think she has come from? All the winter her body has been covered with a hard gum, which spread over it when she wriggled out of her caterpillar skin, and fastened herself by silken threads to the stem of an old cabbage stalk, or hid perhaps in a crack in the palings.

Now that the sun is warm she has come out to lay her eggs. She does not feed on cabbages herself, she sips honey from the flowers. But she fed on leaves when she was a caterpillar, so she lays her eggs under a cabbage leaf, where the caterpillars will find food when they are hatched.

The Tortoiseshell Butterfly, out in the fields, lays her eggs on stinging nettles, because her caterpillars feed on nettle leaves. They weave a little tent under the leaves to come back to at night, and there you may find them.

But if you want to save your cabbages from being eaten by caterpillars, you must look for the eggs of the white cabbage butterfly under the cabbage leaves. They are very tiny, but in a fortnight they will hatch out into little green caterpillars with black spots, and a yellow line down their backs.

They eat and eat for about a month, and then about July or August they creep away to some tree or paling, and bind themselves there by their silken thread till next spring. Then each butterfly comes out to lay her eggs on fresh cabbages.

If you search very carefully all about your garden and in the shed, and along the palings in the winter, you may find and destroy the chrysalis and help to save your cabbages from the caterpillars.

But if you see some little white balls, about the size of a hemp-seed, lying near a dead caterpillar, take care not to destroy them. They are the cocoons of a little fly, which lays her egg in the body of the caterpillar of the white cabbage butterfly, and when the egg is hatched the grub feeds upon the inside of the caterpillar.

Is it not a curious history? The butterfly sucks honey from the flowers, and carries their pollen-dust for them. Then she lays her eggs under a cabbage leaf and dies. The caterpillar feeds on the cabbage, and then perhaps a little fly comes, and lays her egg in him; and the grub feeds on him, so that when the time comes for him to turn into a butterfly he dies instead.

Many other creatures feed on our cabbage. Slugs and snails like green meat and the gall weevil, which we saw feeding on the turnip, likes cabbage

Plant Life in Field and Garden

root as well. The best way to keep all enemies away is to make the ground clean and free from weeds, and to pick off all the insects you find.

Find any Crucifers (flowers formed in a cross) you can—wallflower, candytuft, stock, charlock, turnip, and any cabbage plant which is run to seed. Try to find the chrysalis of the cabbage butterfly.

CHAPTER IX: How Plants Defend Themselves

IN May the hedgerows will be full of flowers. I have not room to describe them all to you. You should pick one of each, on your way to school, and ask your teacher about them. On the tops of the banks, and nestling in the wood, you will find the wild hyacinths, which children call bluebells, and the red ragged-robin, and the lovely starworts or stitchworts with flowers like pure white stars and narrow pointed leaves. Children call these "snap-jacks," because the seed-box, when it is ripe, snaps if you pinch it. There are many kinds of starworts. One of them with small flowers is called chickweed.

The meadows are now golden with buttercups, and the ditches are blue with forget-me-nots, and you can find the little blue Speedwell or Bird's-eye almost anywhere. It is a weed, with thin weak stalks, and you may know it by its four blue petals, and its *two* stamens standing out like horns. Before long the tall Meadow-sweet, with its clusters of tiny white flowers, will be blooming by the side of the streams and in damp places; and the pretty little Bird's-foot Trefoil will brighten the hedgerows and fields.

You will know this little flower well. It grows quite low down, and is like a very small yellow pea-flower. About four or five little blossoms grow on the top of each flower-stalk, and the buds have bright red streaks upon them. When the pods are ripe they stand out like the toes of a bird's foot.

These, and many other flowers, you can find in the fields and hedges and you know now how to look for their seed-boxes and dust-bags; and I am sure you will watch to see what flies and bees and beetles come to fetch honey and pollen-dust.

If you do this and keep your eyes open, you will find out that other creatures come to the plants and flowers, which are not as useful to them as the bees. There is the cow, which takes large mouthfuls of their leaves as she grazes. There is the donkey, which feeds on the thistles. There is the rabbit, which comes out in the evening, to nibble at the tender young shoots; and there are the little field-mice, which scrape away the earth and feed on the thick stems and roots underground.

Plant Life in Field and Garden

Now let me tell you of a few plants which protect themselves, and perhaps you can find more. First come the Anemone and the meadow Buttercup. Both these have bitter leaves which burn your tongue when you bite them. If you walk across a field which has many buttercups in it you will find that the cows and the sheep have left them alone as much as they can. If they eat the leaves, they will not touch the flowers, which are much the most acrid. So these plants prevent the cows from killing them. In the same way the leaves of wild geraniums have a disagreeable taste and smell.

Then there are the Ferns. They have a great deal of bitter tannin in them. You will find that if cows or sheep have been feeding where the Bracken fern is growing, they will not have touched it. So the ferns keep themselves safe.

Then the little Wood-sorrel tastes acid, and the Speedwells dry up the inside of your mouth if you eat their leaves. So these plants are left alone. Lastly the Parson-in-the-pulpit has such poisonous berries, leaves, and underground stems, that no animal will eat it above ground, and no sensible field-mouse would think of nibbling at it underground.

Then there are the plants which grow thorns on their stems. Cows and horses do not like to eat gorse for it hurts their tender mouths. These are a few examples. I cannot give you more, because I want to tell you of something even more curious.

Plants want bees and flies to visit their flowers, because they carry their pollen from flower to flower. But other insects, such as ants and spiders, like honey too, and they only crawl; they rub off any dust which falls on them before they reach another flower. So they rob the flowers of their honey and do nothing in return.

How do you think the plants protect themselves? In many different ways. The Teasel has a large flower-head full of honey. But the ants cannot steal it because its leaves grow opposite to each other on the stem, and join round it so that they make a little basin. The dew and the rain collect in the basin, and stop the ants from creeping past.

Then the plants we call Campions, of which the ragged-robin is one, often have their flower stems covered with fine hairs, and the stem near the flower is very sticky. When the ants climb up to try to steal the honey they stick fast, and can get no further. This is why some of the campions are often called "catch-flies."

1. RAGGED ROBIN; 2. SUN-SPURGE; 3. TEASEL

A very common plant in the hedges is the Sun-spurge, which has curious small green flowers. This plant has a poisonous milky juice in its stem. When the ants try to climb up, they prick holes with their claws, and stick fast and die.

I wish I could tell you more of the way in which plants protect themselves by prickles, by hairs, and by poisons, but you must look for yourselves.

Bring in sun-spurge, campion or catch-fly, wood-sorrel, bracken, teasel, and wild geranium.

CHAPTER X: Wild Flowers and Garden Flowers

NOW you know how wild plants grow, how insects help to make the seeds, and how plants have to defend themselves from enemies which would eat their leaves or steal their honey.

Next let us look at the flowers in our gardens and see how far they are like the wild ones in the fields. All garden plants grow wild in some part of the world. We have taken them into our gardens, and made their flowers larger and brighter. Some still live wild in England, others have been brought from foreign countries.

The forget-me-nots in the garden border are very much the same as those we find in the lanes. The snowdrop has run wild in many parts of England. The lovely blue periwinkle, with its dark shiny leaves, grows in every Devonshire lane. The large ox-eye daisies which grow in our gardens are the same as those in the cornfields. The honey-suckle is as fine in the hedges as on the trellis-work of the porch.

But the large purple clematis and the beautiful yellow and white chrysanthemums, which grow in so many cottage gardens, come from abroad. I knew an old woman once who called them "Christmas anthems." I think she imagined that they flowered late in the year on purpose for Christmas.

The lovely yellow and purple pansies, which bloom all the summer, seem at first too grand to have come from wild ones. But you can gather small wild pansies in the lanes, and if you look inside the flower of the garden pansy you will see the curious bird's head on the top of its seed-box which we found in the violet. So the pansy, or Heartsease, is a true English plant.

I am sure you have some of the yellow and brown polyanthus in your garden. At first you will think there is nothing like it in the fields. But if you gather a cowslip and compare it with the polyanthus, you will find that all their parts are alike. For the polyanthus was once wild like the cowslip, and the gardeners have manured it, and chosen out the best seeds, till they have given it the bright colours it has now.

Plant Life in Field and Garden

WILD PANSY AND GARDEN PANSY

The reason that garden flowers are often larger and more beautiful in their colours than wild flowers is because the plants are not obliged to take so much pains to live nor to make so many seeds. The gardener puts them in good ground, feeds them well, and picks out the seeds of the best flowers to sow next year.

You can do the same if you try, and though you cannot do much in a few years you will get much finer flowers for your trouble. You must watch the plant and pick off all the withered leaves, and keep the ground raked, well manured, and free from weeds. Then you must settle which of the plants have the best and brightest flowers. Tie a little piece of cotton round the stem of these flowers, and watch when their seed-boxes are ripe, then keep these seeds to sow next year. In two or three years you will have much better flowers.

The pinks and carnations are some of the prettiest and sweetest of our garden flowers. They belong to an English family, called the Pink Family. You may perhaps not have any wild pinks in your part of the country. But you will have the ragged robin and the campion, and these belong to the same family.

If you compare their flowers with the pink, you will find that they both have narrow leaves growing opposite each other. The stem is swollen at the joint where they grow. They both have a long green cup with points, and five pink or white petals, ragged at the edge. Ten stamens grow inside on the top of the stem, and there is a tall seed-box in the middle, with two or three sticky horns.

Now try to find a ripe seed-box. It will be open at the top and its points bend out like the top of a vase. Inside is a little upright pillar with the seeds growing round it. When you find all this in a flower you will know that it belongs to the Pink Family.

Chickweed, starwort, campion, soapwort, ragged robin, and wild pink can all be found in the lanes.

But no doubt you have in your garden some double flowers—pinks, wallflowers, stocks, and roses. These have a great many coloured petals, and hardly any dust-bags or seed-box, sometimes none at all. Gardeners have made these double flowers by growing the plants in very rich earth, and sowing the seeds of those which grew the most flower-leaves instead of stamens.

Plants in the fields hardly ever have double flowers. They must make plenty of seeds. If you turn a plant with double flowers out into poor ground and let it run wild, it will go back to single flowers. But gardeners want fine blooms. So they grow double hollyhocks, dahlias, peonies, and primroses, as well as single ones.

Plant Life in Field and Garden

Compare wild and garden rose, wild and garden pansy, cowslip and polyanthus, pink and ragged robin.

CHAPTER XI The Rose Family and its Fruits

IN June the, dog-roses are in bloom. They look very pretty thrusting their pink and white flowers out of the hedge. Though they have thorns, you can manage to cut a branch and take it to school. We will learn to-day about the rose family.

I shall want you to bring a good many flowers and fruits from the hedges and the garden, besides the rose. You remember that some of our best *vegetables* come from the flowers shaped like a cross. Now you will see that some of our best *fruits* come from the Rose Family.

So bring from the hedges a branch of wild rose. It must be wild, for you remember our garden roses have turned most of their stamens into flower leaves. Next get if you can a piece of bramble with a blackberry flower on it. Then from the bank below bring a wild strawberry plant. Get one if you can with a ripe strawberry hanging on it, as well as the flower. For there is another plant called the potentilla which is so like the wild strawberry that you might bring it by mistake, unless you saw the little strawberry fruit.

Then bring from your garden a strawberry, a raspberry, a cherry, and a plum, a green apple and a pear. What a number we shall have! And yet you might bring a peach, a medlar, a quince, a nectarine, and an apricot as well, for all these fruits belong to the Rose Family. Only I expect you will not have them in your garden.

First let us look at the flowers. You will see that the Wild Rose has a very deep cup, with five green sepals, which stick out in long points.

If it is a dog-rose its crown will be made of five lovely pink petals. They are all separate, so that you can pull each one off the green cup, without disturbing the others. If you pull them all off, you will find that there are a great many dust-bags growing on the rim of the green cup.

FRUITS OF THE ROSE FAMILY

Now look for the seed-boxes. Their sticky tops are peeping out of the cup. But you will have to tear the cup open to find them inside. Then you will see that they are all separate and that each one has a sticky top of its own.

Now look at the Strawberry flower: it too has five green sepals and five white petals, and a great many dust-bags, just like the rose. But it has no deep cup. Its seed-boxes grow on a little mound inside the sepals. By-and-by this mound will swell and grow soft and juicy and sweet, and the tiny seed-boxes will be buried in it, like pins in a pincushion. Look at the little fruit of the wild strawberry and the big fruit of the garden strawberry and you will see this. People often call these dry pips "seeds," but they are not seeds, they are tiny seed-boxes, each with one seed inside.

Now look at the Blackberry flower. It is just like the strawberry, and its seed-boxes grow on a mound. But when the fruit is ripe, you will find that the mound is no bigger. In the blackberry, the seed-boxes themselves grow soft, and become small balls full of sweet juice. You can separate them one from another, and you will find a seed inside each.

The Raspberry is like the blackberry, only the little red juicy seed-boxes shrink away from the mound. So you can pull them off like a cap, leaving the white pointed mound behind.

And now how about the other fruits? Next spring when the Plum trees and Cherry trees are in bloom, you will find that they have the same kind of flowers as the rose. But they have only one seed-box to each flower. This seed-box grows juicy outside, and leaves a very hard shell inside, round the seed. So you have to eat the juicy covering and crack the hard shell before you can get at the kernel or seed.

The Apple and the Pear will puzzle you, till you cut an apple across. Then you will see the five little seed-boxes arranged like a star in the middle of the fruit. Each seed-box will have one or two pips or seeds in it, and the boxes are what we call the core of the apple. The green cup has grown thick and fleshy all round them. You can see the dried tips of the green sepals on the top of the apple. In the apple blossom the seed-boxes are separate, till the cup grows round them, and makes one big apple.

Bring a wild rose, a piece of blackberry in flower, a wild strawberry in flower, an apple, pear, plum, cherry, raspberry and garden strawberry.

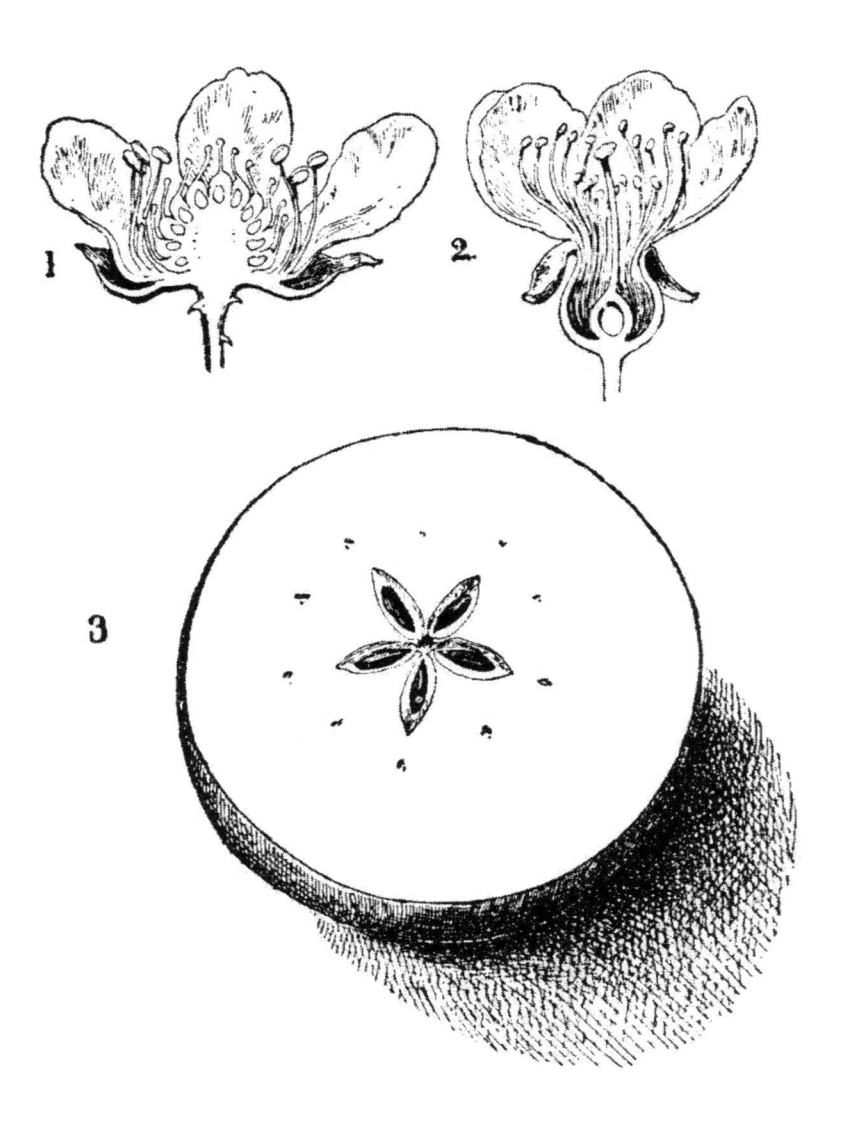

1. BLACKBERRY FLOWER; 2. CHERRY FLOWER; 3. APPLE

CHAPTER XII: The Dead-Nettle and the Pea-Flower

WHEN a bee goes in search of honey, there is one plant she is very glad to find. This is the Dead-nettle. She does not mind whether it has white or purple flowers. She knows that unless some other bee has been there before her she will find some honey.

There are generally plenty of dead-nettles to be found, for their leaves do not taste nice, and they look so like stinging-nettles that very few animals will eat them.

The real nettle has only small green flowers, while the dead-nettle has clusters of red or white blossoms growing all round the stem, just above each pair of leaves. These flowers are shaped like helmets, and they have a broad lip hanging down in front, which has a deep notch in the middle.

The stem of the plant is not round, like the stems of most plants. It is square with four sides. By this you may always know it from a stinging-nettle, even when it is not in flower. The coarse leaves grow opposite to each other, and each pair grows across the one below it, as we saw in Lesson II.

Now let us look at the flower. You had better take a white dead-nettle, as the flowers are large. Take hold of the helmet and pull it very gently. It will come off, leaving the green cup with its five points. But most likely you will have brought away the long tube with sticky horns, which grows out of the seed-box, for it comes off very easily.

If you have, try another flower, and tear the helmet open very carefully. Then you will see that at the bottom of the cup there are four little seed-boxes, like nuts, with a long tube standing right up in the middle of them. It has two sticky horns.

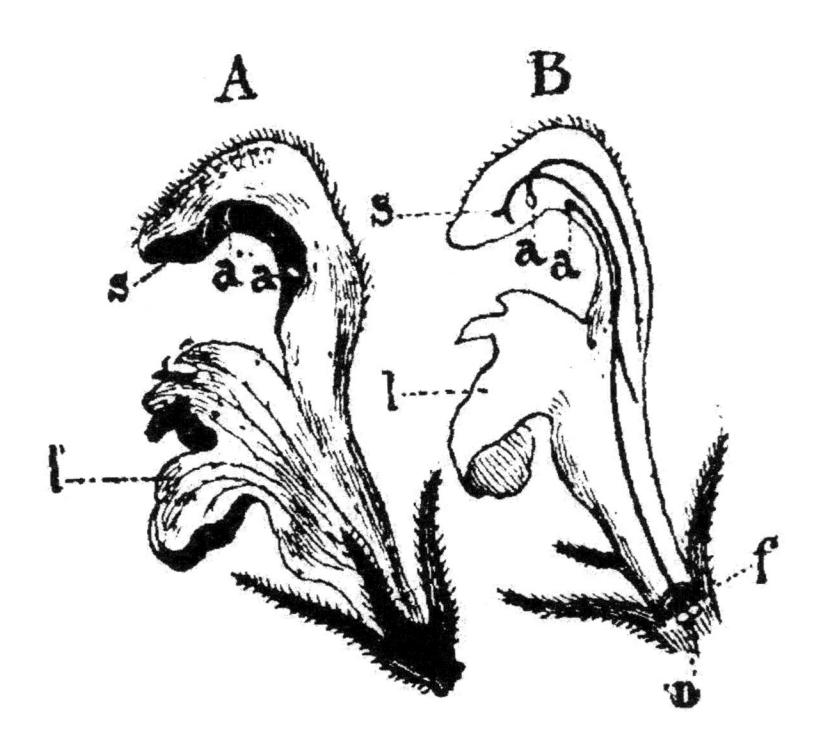

(A) FLOWER OF THE DEAD-NETTLE; (B) FLOWER CUT IN HALF

Now look inside another flower. You will find four stamens growing on the crown, and two of them are so long that they reach right up into the hood. Before you pulled the hood off the sticky horns were close to them. At the bottom of the tube there is plenty of honey, but creeping insects cannot get it, for there is a thick fringe of hairs in the tube to keep them away.

But when the bee comes for honey, she pushes her trunk through the hairs, and as she sucks she brushes the dust out of the bags. Then she goes to another flower and leaves it on the sticky horns. There are a great many flowers with lips like the dead-nettle. Mint, Sage, Balm, Thyme, Peppermint, Lavender, Rosemary, and the pretty blue and white bugle flowers in the hedges are all lipped—you will know them by their square stems, opposite leaves, and the four little seed-boxes.

In Sage plants the anthers swing on a bar. The bee hits her head against the lower end, which is empty, and the full dust-bag comes down on her back.

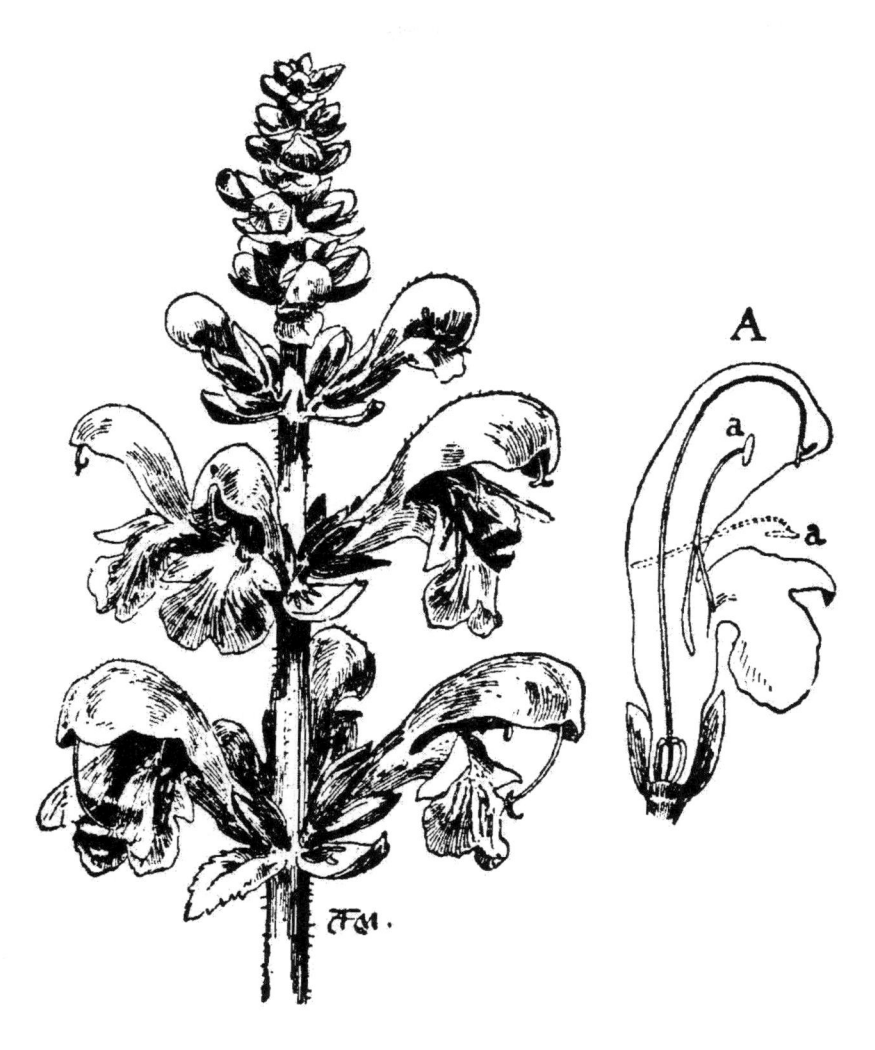

BEES IN MEADOW-SAGE

Another flower which the bee loves is the Pea. There again she is sure to find honey. In the kitchen garden on a fine morning you will see the bees buzzing along the rows of peas and beans, and only stopping to poke their heads into the flowers.

Get a pea-flower and let us see how they do it. Hold the flower facing you. At the back is one large petal, with a deep dent in the middle. This stands up like a flag to tell the bee where to come for honey. So it is called the "standard." Two smaller petals are folded together, just below it. These are called "wings." Between these wings are two more petals, which are joined together like the end of a boat. These are called the "keel."

If you take hold of the wings, and pull them gently down, you will find they bring the keel with them. Then you will see the dust-bags of ten stamens and the sticky beak of the tiny pea-pod. These were hidden before in the keel.

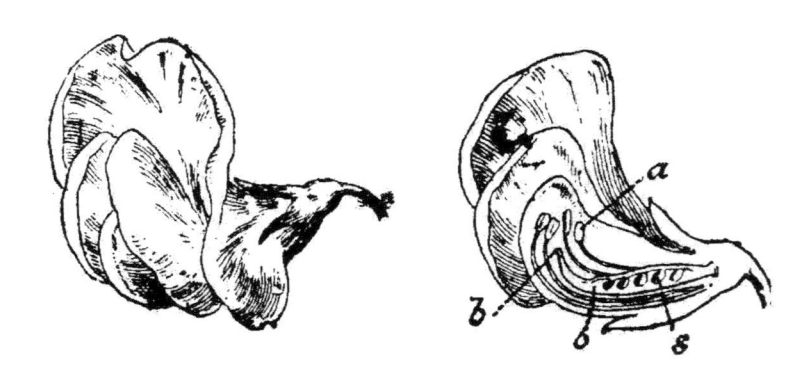

PEA-FLOWER AND SECTION

If you pick the flower to pieces, you will see why the keel came down. Inside each wing there is a knob, which fits into a hollow in the side of the keel. Is not this curious? When the bee settles on the wings, she presses them down with her weight. They press down the keel, and the dust-bags knock against the breast of the bee. So she goes away to the next flower covered with pollen-dust.

There are almost as many flowers like the pea as there are like the dead-nettle. The beautiful yellow Gorse, the little Trefoil, and all the Vetches in the hedges belong to this family. So do the sweet Clovers which we grow for clover hay. Each head of clover is a cluster of tiny flowers shaped like a pea.

Then in the flower garden ee have the Laburnum, and in the kitchen garden the Scarlet-runners and the Broad Beans.

Examine a dead-nettle, mint, thyme, and meadow-sage. Notice the curious swinging anther of the meadow-sage. Also a pea blossom, gorse blossom, tare, and bird's-foot trefoil.

CHAPTER XIII: Climbing Plants

WHEN you were picking the flowers of the peas and scarlet-runners, if you kept your eyes open, you must have noticed that they climb up the sticks which we put for them. But I daresay you did not ask yourself *why* they climb, nor *how* they climb.

You know that if you took the sticks away they would fall in a tangled mass on the ground. For peas and scarlet-runners have thin weak stems. They could not get enough light and air all tumbled together on the ground. They would be stifled under other plants. So they have learnt to climb up on a hedge or sticks, or anything they can find, to lift them towards the sky.

That is why they climb, now let us see how they do it. For they do not both set to work in the same way.

You will find on the pea-plant that in many places where a leaf ought to be, there is a little curled green thread, which clings round the twig of the stick, just as a baby clings to its mother's finger. We call these threads "tendrils." They hold the plant up to the light and air, and let the blossoms hang out where the bees can find them. The scarlet-runners do their climbing differently. They do not use their leaves, but twine their whole stem round the sticks.

PEA CLIMBING BY TENDRILS

If you look along the hedges you will find many climbing plants, which manage to use the thick bushes as a sort of bank on which to spread out their leaves and flowers. There is the Clematis, or Traveller's Joy. It has not turned its leaves into tendrils, nor twined its stem. It twists the stalk of the leaves tightly round the twigs, so that the leaves stand out at the end. Its

Plant Life in Field and Garden

pretty greenish flowers are spread in this way all over the top of the hedge, and by-and-by the feathery seed-boxes will hang like an old man's beard, just where the wind can catch them to blow them away.

1. WILD CLEMATIS, OR TRAVELLER'S JOY; 2. GARDEN PURPLE CLEMATIS

I think you must know the Goose-grass or Cleavers, which grows over everything in the lanes. Its narrow green leaves are arranged round the stem like a star, and it has very tiny white flowers. The stem, leaves and seed-boxes are all crowded with tiny hooks so that it clings to your hand when you gather it. It is really a very weak plant, but it clings to other plants which are stronger, and so raises itself up.

GOOSE-GRASS

The blackberry and other brambles climb in the same way, and the wild rose climbs by its thorns. Further along the hedgerow the wild Hop may be growing. Its stems die down every year and grow up again in the spring.

Yet it manages to spread a long way, for its stem twines round twigs and small trees, and everything it can find, spreading out its broad leaves shaped like a heart. You will find the flowers of the hop rather puzzling, for its dust-bags and seed-boxes grow on different plants.

The Honeysuckle, too, twines its stem, as you must have seen on the porch or the paling. Sometimes when it twines round a young branch, it winds itself so tightly that the branch cannot grow in the places where the honeysuckle binds it. So it is marked all the way up, as if it had a ribbon round it.

HONEYSUCKLE TWINING ROUND A STEM

Then there are the pretty plants called Tares or vetches, which have flowers like small pea-flowers. They climb everywhere by their tendrils. I think you will be able to find all these as well as the Convolvulus or bindweed, which twines round all plants, even our gooseberry and currant bushes, and wants weeding out very carefully. But I am not quite sure whether you can find a curious plant called the Dodder. You must look for it on the common, climbing over the heath and gorse bushes. It is only a thin wiry stem, with clusters of tiny pink flowers on it. It has no leaves at all. How then can it live since it has no leaves to make food? It twines round the gorse, or heath, or clover, and sends its roots into their stems and sucks out ready-made food!

The Vine and the pretty Virginia creepers turn their small branches into threads for climbing. Very likely you have a Virginia creeper on your wall, which turns red in the autumn. Two kinds of this creeper have a very curious plan for climbing. When the threads, or tendrils, touch the wall, their tips turn red, and swell into little cushions. These cushions stick so fast to the wall that even when the branch is dead you have to pull them off. Lastly the Ivy climbs by small roots, which grow all along the stems.

Now you know all the four dodges which plants have for climbing. By hooks, by threads, by their roots, and by the whole plant twining itself round. Try to see how many you can find.

Bring one of each kind of climbing plant.

CHAPTER XIV: How Plants Store Food

SOME plants live for one year only. Some live for two years. Some live for many years.

Have you not noticed that you have to sow mignonette, marigolds, and peas and beans fresh every year in the garden?—unless you keep the young seedlings, which grow from the seeds that fall. In the fields, wheat and oats only live till their grains are ripe, and then die away if they are left in the ground till winter comes.

In the same way chickweed, the corn poppy, and our old friend the shepherd's purse die when their seeds are ripe. These plants are like people who earn just enough to live from day to day, and cannot save for next year.

But if you want to have Sweet Williams, or Canterbury Bells in flower in the summer, you must sow the seeds the summer before. For these plants do not flower the first year. They only grow their root, and a short stem with leaves on it. The plant is busy making food, and storing it up in the root and stem, as starch and sugar and gum, so that it is ready to make a strong flowering plant next year.

Then after they have flowered and made their seeds, these plants die. They have only stored enough for a short life, and cannot live another year. Foxgloves, Thistles, and Wild Parsley behave in this way.

Lastly, you know that Snowdrops, Crocuses, Daisies, Primroses, Pansies, and Dahlias live on for many years, dying down in the autumn and coming up again in the spring. These plants send down the starch and sugar into the root, or the lower part of the stem, or into the bottom of the leaves underground.

Some of them grow more than two years before they try to flower. They are like people who save when they are young, and always go on saving, so that they have something to spare.

You can sometimes make a plant store up food. If you sow some mignonette and put one plant in a pot, and keep on nipping off the flower-buds so that it cannot make seeds, it will grow into a little shrub, and flower for two or three years.

Plant Life in Field and Garden

Different plants store their food in different parts. The wild carrot and the acorn, which is growing into an oak, store theirs in the root. The carrot is fleshy and only lasts two years. But the root of the oak is woody and lives long.

The lesser celandine, you remember, stores its food in small white lumps like white sugar-plums, which are swollen roots with a bud at the top. The marsh marigolds, and the pretty yellow flags, which grow by the river, store theirs in an underground stem. You must follow the stalks of the marsh marigold right back till you come close to the roots, and there you will find the thick knob, which lives on, all through the winter, and sends up fresh leaves in the spring.

If you can get a long piece of the creeping stem of the yellow flag, you will see the marks of the places where the flowering stems have come up year after year. They follow each other along the stem till you come to the plant of this year. And beyond that is the bud for next year.

There is a very pretty plant called Solomon's Seal, which is wild in some parts of England, and is often grown in cottage gardens. It has a tall flower-stalk with rather narrow leaves, and lovely white flowers, with green tips, The flowers hang down all on one side of the stalk. If you dig up a piece of the stem of this plant you will see large scars like seals upon it. These are the places where the stems have grown year after year, and this is why it is called Solomon's Seal.

PRIMROSE AND SOLOMON'S SEAL

You can make out for yourself the mass of stems and buds people call a primrose root. I want now to show you an underground *bud* or bulb. Dig up a wild hyacinth, usually called a blue-bell. You will find that it has a large knob at the bottom, with small roots growing out of it. Cut this knob in half,

Plant Life in Field and Garden

and notice that it is a bulb made of scaly leaves folded one over the other, exactly like an onion.

It you dig it up in the spring, the flower-stalk will be standing up in the middle, and when you pull the scaly leaves off one by one, you will find another bud *very small* close to the bottom of the flower-stalk. If you dig up another plant in the autumn, the flower-stalk will have withered away, and the baby bud will be peeping out of the top of the bulb.

This is what has happened. After the hyacinth left off flowering, the leaves grew long and made food and sent it down to the scaly leaves underground. The bulb grew fat and strong, and the small bulb inside grew larger. Now it is ready to lie quiet all the winter. When the spring comes the little bulb will take the food from the thick scaly leaves, and grow into a new plant.

Bring six plants—two with food stored in the root, two in the underground stem, two in bulbs.

CHAPTER XV: Underground Vegetables

NOW you will be able to understand how it is that we get such nourishing vegetables from the kitchen garden. The bees take honey and pollen from the *flowers* of plants. We take the sugar and starch and other food, which they store up in their *leaves*, and *stems*, and *roots*.

Carrots, Parsnips, and Beet-roots are plants which store up food in their roots the first year, and flower the second year. So we sow them, and feed them very well the first year, and when they have laid up a good store of sweet food, we pull them up and eat them before they can flower.

If you can get your father to leave one of these plants in the ground till the second year, you will see it flower and make its seeds. But a turnip will flower in the first year, if you sow it early in the spring, and leave it all the summer. This is why we sow our largest stock of turnips in June and July so that they may not flower before we want them in the winter.

Now I think I hear a little boy saying, "She has forgotten potatoes." No, I have not. But potatoes are not roots, like carrots and turnips. Cut one open and you will see some dark spots in it called "eyes." Indeed you may see them without cutting if you wash it and look carefully.

Each of these eyes is a little bud, with a growing tip, and the beginning of leaves. Now you know that a root cannot bear leaves. It can only have one bud on the top where the stem begins. So the Potato cannot be a root.

Neat time you dig up some potatoes for dinner, look at the roots carefully before you shake off the potatoes. You will then see that each potato grows at the end of a white stalk, very different from the roots. For a potato is a swelling at the end of a stem, which grows underground. It is a "tuber" like the Jerusalem Artichokes, which I expect you also have in the garden.

If you cut up either an artichoke or a potato into pieces, and leave a bud in each piece, it will grow up into a new plant, and send down food into the stems below the ground, and form more tubers. The potato plant flowers, and forms seed every year. The seed-box is poisonous, and so are the seed-boxes of many of the Potato Family. The Deadly Nightshade, with its dark

Plant Life in Field and Garden

black berries, belongs to this family. It is never safe to eat any berry, or other fruit, unless you know what it is, for many berries which even the birds eat, are poisonous to some animals and to man.

The potato plant stores its poison only in its seed-box, which is green, there is none in the potato. The potato disease which gives us so much trouble is a little plant like the mould on jam, which eats the potato away.

In Celery we eat the stems which grow above ground. But we earth them up to keep them white. For plants cannot become green without sunlight. In Asparagus we eat the green stem with the bud at the top. Those buds which we do not eat branch out in summer, and have beautiful leaves and bright red berries.

Lastly in Onions, Leeks, and Shallots we eat the bulbs, or underground buds, like that of the hyacinth. They have plenty of good food in them stored up in the scaly leaves.

Now let us see what you must do if you want your roots, bulbs, and stems to grow into good vegetables. First you must drain the ground if it wants it, and dig it deeply and break the earth up so that the roots have no hard lumps in their way and can grow straight and strong. Then you must dig in some manure. And be careful that you dig it in deep, for grubs and maggots like carrots and onions as much as we do; and in the autumn and spring, when you dig the garden, they are lying about in their cocoon shells. If you bury them deeply in the ground, then when they turn into flies they cannot get out to lay eggs.

There is another way in which you can get the better of them. Each plant has its own grub which feeds upon it. There is the grub of the onion fly, of the carrot fly, and so on. So when you sow your seed, if you sow the carrots where the onions were last year, and the onions in the old parsnip bed, when the fly is hatched she does not find the leaves for her eggs close at hand, and you may save your roots.

Then in such plants as carrots and onions you must keep the roots and bulbs well covered, and when you thin them out you must make the ground firm again. For the onion fly and the carrot fly lay their eggs *on* the root or bulb), and if they cannot find their way in, the root is safe.

Bring six vegetables—1. root; 2. bulb; 3. stem; 4. tuber; 5. leaves; 6, flowers.

UNDERGROUND VEGETABLES

Lastly, you know the troublesome wireworm which wriggles along just underground and eats everything it finds. To be even with him you must keep the ground clean, for he likes rubbish to hide in, and you had better mix some salt or lime with the earth. If he is still troublesome you can put some slices of potato just under the ground and stick a twig in, to show where they are, and you are pretty sure to find him underneath in the early morning.

CHAPTER XVI: How Seeds Travel

IN the autumn, when the plants have left off flowering, there is plenty for us to do in looking for fruits, and finding out how they scatter their seeds.

Some drop them near at home. The poppy, as we saw, has a hard fruit with little openings under the cover. When the stalk bends the seeds fall out through these holes and grow in the ground all around.

If you look at the dry seed-boxes of the wild geranium which grows in the lanes, you will see that each one has curled up from the bottom. There will be five little curls round the sticky knob in the middle, and the seeds will be gone.

There is a tall yellow Balsam which is found wild in some parts of England, and another with reddish flowers, which is often grown in cottage gardens, which have a most amusing seed-box. When it is ripe it bursts open and flings out its seeds. If you can get a friend to touch a ripe pod, it will make you laugh to see how he jumps as it pops with a bang in his hand. This is why the plant is often called "touch-me-not."

But plants want their seeds to be carried farther away than even popping will send them. Think how many flowers there are crowded together in a hedgerow. If all the seeds fell close round they would stifle each other. So plants try all sorts of plans to get their seeds scattered.

I am sure you have blown the feathery dandelion "clocks" on your way home from school. Next time you do it look at one of the little floating messengers. Do you remember that when we looked at the dandelion we found that it was a flower-head with hundreds of tiny flowers, and that each flower had an oval seed-bag at the bottom with a number of fine hairs on the top of it and a yellow crown with a long strap?

Now the yellow crown has withered away, and the top of the seed-box his grown up into a long neck with the hairy sepals on the top. And when the wind catches these hairs it carries the tiny fruit along perhaps for miles, and then it drops down to grow.

Thistles and sow-thistles, groundsel and teasels, and a number of other flowers of that kind have these feathery seeds. So you see when you let them grow on your own ground you spoil the ground of other people as well.

This is the way that *wind* carries seeds.

Other seeds are washed down by streams and left on their banks. Others, again, are often carried in the mud that sticks to the feet of birds.

Another plan is to grow tiny hooks on the seed-boxes so that animals carry them. The goose-grass does this. We saw on that it has tiny hooks all over its stem and leaves, which it uses for climbing. It has the same kind of hooks on its tiny seeds. If you take a bunch of goose-grass in your hand you will get a number of the very small seed-boxes sticking to your fingers.

But there is a much bigger "burr," which grows on the common Burdock in the lanes. The burdock is a tall plant, with very large heart-shaped leaves and pink flower-heads, something like a thistle. You often bring its burrs home on your clothes, dogs carry them in their hair, and sheep in their fleece. Each of these burrs is a cup of leaves covered with hooks. The leaves grow together into a ball with the flowers peeping out at the top, and if you open a ripe burr you will find the tiny fruit inside.

So you, and the dogs, and the sheep carry the seeds for the plants.

But the prettiest plan of all is when the seed-box grows into a sloe, or a cherry, or into some bright berry like the berries of the hawthorn and the honeysuckle. For then the birds come to eat the nice fruit, and when they carry it off to some tree near they drop the stone down in a new place. Or they eat the berry, and the hard seeds pass through their body, and fall with their droppings somewhere far off.

Now you see why the blackberry and the raspberry grow juicy pulp round their seeds, and why the little hard seed-boxes of the strawberry stick in the juicy mound. All this is to tempt the birds to eat them and carry their seeds.

So too in the hip of the wild rose, the green cup grows large and soft, and turns a bright red just when winter is coming, and there is not much food. Then the birds come and peck at the cup, and the seed-boxes inside stick to their beaks or are swallowed, and so are carried away.

Plant Life in Field and Garden

1. BURDOCK; 2. WILD GERANIUM

You know that in a hard winter the holly berries and mistletoe, the hips and haws, and even the berries of the yew and the honeysuckle, are often all gone before Christmas. But I daresay you did not know before that the birds were carrying about seeds to grow up next year.

But if you keep your eyes open, you can learn a great many things like these, which children shut up in towns cannot see. You are happy to live in the beautiful country, among the birds and the flowers. You breathe the fresh air, which the plants make sweet, you gather your own flowers, and grow your own vegetables and fruit, and you can watch the plants in your garden growing prettier every year.

Try to find the fruits of the wild geranium, yellow balsam, dandelion, groundsel, thistle, teasel, goose-grass, burdock, rose, hawthorn, honeysuckle, yew, and other plants.

Made in the USA
Lexington, KY
30 March 2018